GOD'S MASTER KEY
TO PROSPERITY

BY GORDON LINDSAY

Published By
CHRIST FOR THE NATIONS INC.
Dallas, Texas
Sixth Reprint 1998

CONTENTS PAGE

Introduction

Is it the will of God for His people to have material prosperity in this world? Is it in accordance with His plan that they have large possessions of this world's goods? These have long been muted and controversial questions. In fact, there are few questions as important that have been left as open as these. Today, there are deep searchings of the heart among many of God's people for the real truth of the matter.

There are some who would teach that poverty is a blessing. They point out that the disciples who followed Jesus were poor, and at times did not have money to pay a simple tax. They also note that many of the great saints during this age have suffered poverty and hardship. They contend that God's blessing has been upon the poor rather than upon those who have possession of unusual amounts of this world's goods. They point out, moreover, that many of the characters of Old Testament times served the Lord faithfully until they had achieved prosperity, and then they failed God.

However, while it is true that riches have often resulted in people becoming proud and arrogant, yet it is also common knowledge that the poor can be just as deficient in character as the rich. It is a matter of record that out of poverty have arisen many great men. But there have been godly men of wealth also—such as Abraham. It is yet to be proved that either poverty or riches, in themselves, are the final answer to the problem of developing Christian character. But one thing is certain: the right use of wealth is of the utmost importance in the determining of human destiny.

Much has been written about tithing being the key to prosperity. We believe the Bible bears out that the teaching of tithing is sound and scriptural; in this book we have taken consideration of this truth. However, we must add that it is our belief that in general writers have stopped short of the full answer to the question of Christian prosperity. Jesus plainly told of a *master key to material blessings in this world.*

Strangely enough, little has been said or written about this key. Yet just as tithing was the master key in the Old Testament to temporal blessing (and is still important in the New), so there is a master key to prosperity in the New Testament.

One thing we should note. Although Jesus spoke again and again against covetousness, which is the desire for wealth for the purpose of hoarding it, He never said that Christians should avoid material possessions, nor that they should seek poverty for poverty's sake. He did say, "But seek ye first the kingdom of God, and his righteousness; and all these things shall be added unto you" (Matt. 6:33). Jesus taught that first and foremost, it is the responsibility of every human being to seek the kingdom of God. He said, "No man can serve two masters. . . Ye cannot serve God and mammon" (Matt. 6:24).

Nevertheless, the thought is clearly expressed by Jesus that if a man puts God first, then God will put him first. If a man truly seeks the kingdom of God he need not be anxious about the material things of life. God will meet his needs and give him an abundance of material blessings in due time. As John the beloved wrote in his last epistle:" Beloved, I wish above all things that thou mayest prosper and be in health, even as thy soul prospereth" (III John 2). What then is this master key to prosperity? Of that we shall take due note in this book.

CHAPTER 1

The Bible's Great Success Story

As an introduction to our study of the Bible law of prosperity, we shall consider the story of two great Bible characters. The lives of these two men illustrate the working of this divine law of temporal prosperity—how that heeding it brought good success to one, while failure and trouble came to the other who disregarded it.

With the first of these two, the pursuit of wealth had actually little or no place. Nevertheless he became a rich man. Not only did he gain great wealth, but God gave him many years to enjoy his prosperity.

The other man also had faith, although his faith was of a mixed kind. He believed in God, desired His blessings, but at the same time was possessed of a driving ambition to become rich, an ambition he would gratify, if necessary, at the expense of others. The methods that he employed to achieve success have ever since been a classic example of the wrong way to get rich. He did, however, finally learn his lesson, and from that time sought to walk the life of a true pilgrim. God brought him eventually into a place of peace, and during the sunset of his life Jacob enjoyed the blessings of prosperity and of a united family.

God has given us the stories of these two men as examples of the right way and the wrong way to achieve prosperity.

ABRAHAM—FATHER OF THE FAITHFUL

Abraham is indeed a unique Bible character, in that to

an almost equal degree he enjoyed both great spiritual and temporal blessings. He was rich in silver and gold; he was also rich in his knowledge and understanding of Jehovah.

As a reward for his consecration and obedience, God gave promises to Abraham that He gave to no one else. Abraham was to become father of the faithful. Kings were to come from his loins. His seed was to become as the sands of the sea and the stars of the heavens for multitude. He was not only to be blessed, but his obedience was to reach out and bless generations in all ages to come. Let us now seek to discover the secret that made this man's success so great.

ABRAHAM LEFT ALL TO OBEY GOD (Gen. 12)

When God called Abraham, He did not promise him that He was going to prosper his business or show him the way to make a fortune. Instead, God called him to leave all! "Get thee out of thy country, and from thy kindred and from thy father's house, unto a land that I will show thee" (Gen. 12:1). Had Abraham had his eye on becoming wealthy he would no doubt have remained in Haran. Encyclopedia Americana says, "Haran...to the Assyrians was a strategic post of great importance. An extensive commerce centered there."

Apparently Abraham's father, Terah, had accumulated property in Haran. Abraham would have had to remain there to have inherited this property. But God called the patriarch to journey to a land that he had never seen and there to begin a new life. Abraham was more interested in God's inheritance than in that of his father, Terah, who lived in a land of idolatry (Joshua 24:14-15). He was concerned more with that city "whose builder and maker is God" (Heb. 11:10). He made the decision to put God first in everything. And that resolution guided every decision he would make in the future.

And so Abraham, disregarding his prospects in Haran, journeyed on to the land of Canaan. But did Abraham find things inviting when he reached that land? Hardly! He got there at just the time of a great famine! It looked very much as if he had made the greatest mistake of his life. Abraham and his household were scarcely able to find enough to eat. Under pressure of the famine, he journeyed down into Egypt, a place where he soon ran into more difficulties. Everything seemed to go wrong. It must have appeared to those of his company that Abraham had made a serious mistake. Nevertheless, the prophet, neither then nor later, ever allowed himself to doubt God. For him there was no turning back. He had burned the bridges behind him, and he had no intention of returning to Haran. God had told him He would bless and prosper him. Somehow he believed that God's promise would be fulfilled.

ABRAHAM WAS NOTED FOR HIS GENEROSITY
(Gen: 13, 14)

Now Abraham had brought his nephew, Lot, along with him. After Abraham had returned to Canaan, following the famine referred to, he enjoyed a period of real prosperity. His flocks and herds and those of his nephew, Lot, multiplied to such numbers that there was not room for them all to dwell together. At this point in their sojourning, they had come to the borders of a valley in the plain of the Jordan. Although this area around Sodom and Gomorrah was soon to come under divine judgment it was nevertheless at that time "as the garden of the Lord" (Gen. 13:10). It must have seemed a tempting place for Abraham to settle down and make his home. As chieftain of his company, he had the right of first choice. But Abraham saw that Lot desired it and he let him have what he wanted. He himself took the land which his nephew evidently thought was a much less favorable choice than the valley. But neither Abraham nor Lot had any anticipation that even then, the cities of the plains were about to come under divine judgment.

For a time Lot prospered in the plains of Sodom; but one day a war broke out. Some tribal kings came against Sodom because that city had decided it would no longer pay tribute. In the battle, the king of Sodom and his confederate kings were defeated. The invaders gathered up the wealth of the cities that could be carried away and took the inhabitants, including the family of Lot, into captivity—presumably to become slaves. Abraham mobilized his company and pursued them. In the darkness they made a surprise attack, defeating the host of the enemy and recovering the hostages as well as the goods that had been taken.

The king of Sodom offered to make a deal. If Abraham would return the captives he could keep the goods. But Abraham's answer was:

> "I will not take from a thread even to a shoe latchet, and that I will not take any thing that is thine, lest thou shouldest say, I have made Abram rich" (Gen. 14:23).

If God was going to prosper Abraham, He must do it in His own way. Abraham would not have it said that the king of Sodom had made him rich. He knew the exceeding wickedness of that city. Apparently he wanted to have nothing to do with those who lived in those cities. He did not want to be linked up or associated with the king of Sodom in any way.

Abraham was a generous man and given to hospitality, as shown on the occasion when he "entertained angels unawares" (Heb. 13:2 and Gen. 18). He did not gain his wealth by shrewd dealing, by driving sharp bargains with his fellowmen, or by exploiting his office as a prophet.

When Abraham sought a burial place for his wife,

Sarah, he refused the offer of the children of Heth to accept a plot of ground without cost. Abraham knew that the gift was given merely because he was reckoned as a great man (Gen. 23:6). The world always considers it politic to give gifts to important men. Abraham refused the gift, even as he refused everything that belonged to the king of Sodom.

ABRAHAM'S SUPREME TEST (Gen. 22)

But Abraham's great and supreme test came when he was asked to offer up his only son Isaac as a sacrifice. Would even Abraham be able to face and pass such a supreme test of his faith in God? Many would like to share the blessings of Abraham, but would they be willing to pass through the same tests? In observing Abraham's complete surrender to the absolute will of God we shall find the key to the mighty blessings that he received.

The incident of the offering of Isaac has long been one over which the critics have stumbled. We shall briefly take note of this before we consider the lesson that it teaches. The critics' objection is that the incident supposedly teaches the offering of human sacrifice. Actually, as we shall see, it teaches the very opposite!

First, as all Bible readers know, the incident typifies the offering of Christ by the Father for the sins of the world. Abraham in his role as father of Isaac was a type of the Father who "spared not his own Son, but delivered him up for us all" (Rom. 8:32), and Isaac was a type of Christ who was "obedient unto death" (Phil. 2:5-8).

Second, Isaac, in another way, typifies the fallen human race, which in view of divine justice is doomed to die. However, mercy prevailed over justice by providing a substitionary sacrifice in Christ, of which the ram caught in the thicket is the type.

Concerning this supposed objection that the story teaches human sacrifice: actually, the whole incident was

9

God's protest against that heathen custom! In the days of Abraham this cruel practice was widespread. It was extensively practiced by many Canaanite tribes at that time, as the research of modern archeology shows. Abraham was familiar with this heathen ritual and knew that its practice was widespread. He was deeply grieved when God proposed that he offer up Isaac, his son. Yet so deep was his consecration to the will of God that he did not reason nor hestiate to obey what he knew was the voice of God.

But although Abraham did not know it, God had no intention of having Isaac offered up as a human sacrifice. At the last moment the angel of the Lord appeared and directed Abraham's attention to the ram which was to take Isaac's place. Far from teaching human sacrifice, God was taking this occasion to show for all time to come that the practice is wrong and wholly unnecessary. God has provided a substitute sacrifice in Christ, and therefore human beings are never to be so offered. Indeed, such a sacrifice, great as it would cost a parent, could accomplish nothing.

Abraham met the supreme test and passed it with flying colors. He had truly shown that he was willing if need to be to give up all to God, retaining nothing. Because he had withheld nothing, he now became the recipient of the greatest blessing that God could give any man.

> "And he said, Lay not thine hand upon the lad, neither do thou any thing unto him: for now I know that thou fearest God, seeing thou hast not withheld thy son, thine only son from me. . . By myself have I sworn, saith the Lord, for because thou hast done this thing, and hast not withheld thy son, thine only son: That in blessing I will bless thee, and in multiplying I will multiply thy seed as the stars of the heaven, and as the sand which is upon the sea shore; and thy

seed shall possess the gate of his enemies; And in thy seed shall all the nations of the earth be blessed; because thou hast obeyed my voice" (Gen. 22:12, 16-18).

Because Abraham was obedient, God promised him the very gates of the earth, and that his seed would be as the stars of heaven in multitude. Abraham, by giving all, had thus gained all. By leaving all, he had obtained all. By seeking spiritual things he received temporal things also. Here was a man who had learned the secret of receiving both spiritual and temporal blessings.

THE SECRETS OF ABRAHAM'S PROSPERITY

1. Abraham forsook all to obey God.
2. He refused to turn back in the midst of test.
3. He did not seek wealth by sharp practices.
4. He refused the wealth of Sodom (type of the world).
5. He was generous and honest.
6. He met the supreme test of obeying God if it cost him everything.
7. He obeyed the law of the tithe (discussed in chapter 3).

Have you read the story of Abraham carefully? If so, you may have recognized in it the clue to the master key of an abundant prosperity.

Chapter 2

The Man Who Wanted
To Be Rich

Jacob was a man not without faith in God. The Bible speaks of the God of Abraham, Isaac and Jacob. But as we observe the events of his early career, it appears that in marked contrast to Abraham, it was Jacob's desire, more than anything else in the world, to become rich. Jacob had observed how God had prospered his grandfather and he saw and coveted this prosperity. But apparently he knew little or nothing of that supreme consecration that Abraham had made to Jehovah which was the basis of his prosperity. He had little opportunity to cultivate the acquaintance of his grandfather, for he died while Jacob was yet a lad of fifteen. The youth, not knowing the secrets of Abraham's wealth, was fired with an ambition to attain his outward prosperity. In his way of thinking there was one way to secure it, and that was "to get all he could while the getting was good." At the same time he would be a worshipper of Jehovah. He would show that it was possible to serve both God and mammon!

THE BIRTHRIGHT AND THE BLESSING
(Gen. 25-28)

According to custom, the birthright belonged to the eldest son. Jacob and Esau were twins, but Esau was born first, therefore the birthright was his. Jacob considered this a great misfortune, and he began to consider ways and means by which he might get it transferred into his own possession. He decided that the way to accomplish

12

his objective was to wait until Esau was in a desperate plight. He knew his brother loved to hunt and would rather spend his time in that occupation than anything else. But hunting was profitable only when the seasons were favorable. Sometimes there were drouths and the game would retreat to remote parts. Esau did not like farming and had no income from the field to fall back upon. At such a time Jacob foresaw he might be able to drive a hard bargain.

He bided his time, and the day came when Esau returned from the field faint and empty-handed and was—so he thought—about to perish from hunger. Jacob was now ready to make a bargain with him, but only if he would trade him his birthright. In a moment of weakness the bargain was made, which Esau was to regret the rest of his life.

But Jacob was not yet satisfied. He knew that his father, Isaac, intended to bestow a special blessing upon Esau, his elder and favorite son. He coveted that blessing for himself. There was more scheming and planning. With the connivance of his mother, Rebekah, who had some good qualities, yet also seemed to possess a streak of intrigue, the two schemed to get the blessing for Jacob, in addition to the birthright he had already secured. To them the end seemed to justify the means.

When Isaac spoke to his son, Esau, that the time had come to give him the blessing, and while his son went out into the fields to secure savoury meat for him, Jacob and his mother set their plan into operation. A couple of young goats were killed to make a savoury meat. The skins of the kids were put on Jacob's hands and neck to simulate the feel of the skin of Esau. Thus Isaac, deceived as to the identity of the one before him, gave the blessing to Jacob.

But that was far from the end of the story, as we shall

see. Jacob was to pay over and over for his deception. He was forced to leave home. Never again was he to see his mother, Rebekah. His hopes of enjoying the inheritance he had secured by trickery were soon dispelled. He was forced to flee for his life from his enraged brother, Esau. With only what he would carry with him, he made the long journey to his mother's people in far-off Padan-Aram.

SCHEMING IN PADAN-ARAM (Gen. 29-31)

Here in the land of the East, Jacob made his home. Though he had received an experience with God at Bethel, he had not yet given up his shrewd practices. But here he met people who were just as shrewd as he was. He worked in Padan-Aram seven years to secure the wife he loved, but at the end of the time, he found that Laban had craftily interjected a condition into the contract. Pleading the customs of the land, Laban told Jacob that the younger daughter could not be given before the elder (Gen. 29:26). So it was that he had an unwanted wife on his hands, and had to work another seven years to get the one he loved. It was a battle of wits of one trader against another. Jacob apparently had met his match. Laban shortchanged Jacob again and again. Jacob complained to his wives that their father had changed his wages ten times (Gen. 31:7).

In the end, however, Jacob's cunning outwitted the maneuverings of his father-in-law. In connection with an arrangement with Laban, Jacob's discovery of certain biological laws enabled him to secure possession of the stronger of the cattle. In so doing he incurred the animosity of Laban's sons. The time came when Jacob saw that there was mischief on foot against him. He would do as he had done before when trouble came: he would flee. But this time he would see that everything he had secured claim to would be taken with him.

And that is when Jacob's troubles really began. Laban came after him, intending to avenge himself of his troublesome son-in-law. However he was restrained from this, due to divine intervention (Gen. 31:29). Having escaped the danger from the rear, tidings came to Jacob of still graver dangers ahead. He had dared to hope that Esau, by this time, had forgotten the old feud. Apparently he was wrong. The news reached him that Esau was coming against him with 400 men of war (Gen. 32:6). Jacob was alarmed. He realized the signs indicated that his brother was not coming in peace. Not if he was coming to meet him with an army of 400! What should he do? Jacob at last came face to face with reality. There was no running from danger now, for there was no way to run. He had only one last recourse and that was God.

THE CHANGE (Gen. 32)

That night, Jacob went across the brook Jabbok and was left alone. There he wrestled with the angel of God. In the distance he knew that Esau was coming to execute vengeance. No one but God could help him. But in that night of travail a new man was born—Israel, a prince with God! That night Jacob was to learn that there were other things more important than the material things of this world that could so easily be taken from him. For the first time he saw that spiritual things must rank first. God will give His people material blessings, but first they must seek the spiritual. As Jesus said, "Seek ye first the kingdom of God, and his righteousness; and all these things shall be added unto you" (Matt. 6:33).

Jacob won a notable victory that night. He had prevailed with God. When Esau appeared on the scene he was a changed man. Instead of a bloody battle, the two brothers melted into each other's arms. Jacob, instead of scheming to outwit his brother by driving a sharp bargain, wanted to divide his herd with Esau. And Esau, instead of eagerly accepting the gift, had to be urged to accept.

But Jacob had not yet paid the full price of his evil sowing. Years of misdeeds are not expiated in a moment. The foundations of prosperity have to be laid. It was many years before Jacob would have the peace his heart longed for. True, he had the peace that comes from being a believer in Jehovah. But his sons had not learned their lesson. They, like he once was, were carnal, envious, grasping, and even murderous. His favorite wife, Rachel, was a devotee of image worship. Jacob apparently got her to give up her gods and turn to Jehovah (Gen. 35:1-4). But not long after, she died during the birth of their son, Benjamin.

Many other misfortunes befell him. Dinah, his daughter, was violated. Simeon and Levi went on a murderous rampage, taking the lives of many innocent people in a mission to avenge their sister. Reuben committed incest with one of his father's wives. The other sons broke their father's heart by their treacherous conduct in selling their brother, Joseph, into Egypt. Jacob had once deceived his father, Isaac, by killing a kid and using its skin to deceive Jacob. "Whatsoever a man soweth, that shall he also reap" (Gal. 6:7) is an eternal principle that none may ignore with impunity.

However, there came the time when things changed and the last years of Jacob's life were good years. When the change came, it took place suddenly. In the midst of distresses occasioned by the severe famine, came the strange tidings that his son, Joseph, long thought dead, was indeed alive and had been made lord over all the land of Egypt. This was his message to the family of Jacob:

"Now thou art commanded, this do ye; take you wagons out of the land of Egypt for your little ones, and for your wives, and bring your father, and come. Also regard not your stuff; for the good of all the land of Egypt is yours" (Gen. 45:19,20).

Jacob was thus commanded to leave all and come at once to Joseph. All that he could desire in the way of temporal blessings was now his. Jacob had learned his lesson. God gives wealth to His children who will use it for His glory. He may withhold it from those who desperately seek it, or who will not use it for His glory. Material blessings are for believers who seek first the kingdom of God.

IN SEARCH OF GOD

An interesting story is told by Mr. Roger Babson, the famous statistician, of an incident that took place some years ago when he visited Argentina. He said:

"Just before I went to Brazil I was the guest of the President of Argentine Republic. After lunching one day we sat in his sun parlor looking out over the river. He was very thoughtful. He said, 'Mr. Babson, I have been wondering why it is that South America with all its great natural advantages is so far behind North America, notwithstanding that South America was settled before North America.' Then he went on to tell how the forests of South America had two hundred and eighty-six trees that can be found in no book on botany. He told me of many ranches that had thousands of acres planted in alfalfa in one block. He mentioned the mines of iron, copper, coal, silver, gold; all those rivers and great waterfalls which rival Niagara. 'Why is it, with all these natural resources, South America is so far behind North America?' he asked. Well, those of you who have been there know the reason.

"But, being a guest, I said: 'Mr. President, what do you think is the reason?' He replied, 'I have come to this conclusion: South America was settled by the Spanish who came to South America in search of gold, but North America was settled by the Pilgrim Fathers, who went there in search of God.' "

Chapter 3

The Old Testament Key to Prosperity

The first words of the Bible are, "In the beginning God created the heaven and the earth" (Gen. 1:1). Therefore creation belongs to Him and He has the right to ordain the laws by which it is governed. After ordering the earth and providing the conditions that would make it a home for mankind, God created Adam and Eve and made them progenitors of the human race.

THE GARDEN OF EDEN (Gen. 2, 3)

Now the first words which God spoke to man have vital significance to our subject: the law of prosperity. God said:

"Of every tree of the garden thou mayest freely eat:
But of the tree of the knowledge of good and evil,
thou shalt not eat of it: for in the day that thou eatest
thereof thou shalt surely die" (Gen. 2:16, 17).

Here God stated a great principle. He had placed man in the Garden of the Lord and had provided every blessing for his happiness and pleasure. Nothing was required to obtain any of these blessings, temporal or otherwise. All had been freely provided. With one notable exception, it was Adam and Eve's privilege to partake of any tree of the Garden. However, and this was important, there was one tree God had reserved for Himself, and man was to leave it strictly alone—that was the tree of knowledge of good and evil.

Now it was in man's hand to either respect this com-

18

mandment, or to disobey it. But because the fruit of the tree appeared to be good for food, and desirable to make one wise, Adam and Eve chose to accept Satan's lie and disbelieve God. They reached forth their hand and the irrevocable deed was done. The tragic result that followed their fateful act need not be elaborated on. The curse came upon them swiftly and surely. A train of sin, evil, pain, sorrow, sickness and death followed their trail and that of their descendants—a trail of misery and woe that still continues. God had given man every blessing he needed, but had reserved something for Himself. Man violated this law, took what belonged to God, and the curse came upon him. Driven from Eden he had to earn his living by the sweat of his brow. The ground violated the law of prosperity, and now became subject to the law of poverty and death. The fact is that God, in giving His blessings to man, always reserves something for Himself which He requires to be kept inviolate. This brings us to the law of the tithe which is one of the vital keys to the enjoyment of temporal prosperity.

ABRAHAM AND THE TITHE (Gen. 14: 18-24)

The Bible in a few brief chapters relates the events of the first two thousand years of human history. But with the appearance of Abraham (whose experiences we have already recorded) the biblical narrative goes into detail of God's dealings with man. After a sad story of self-will that dominates the scene in both pre and postdiluvian days, there appears this man Abraham who will listen to the voice of God—a man who believed in giving to God what belonged to Him, and who recognized that God was the author of all true prosperity.

In the previous chapter we discussed six of the great rules of prosperity which were demonstrated in the life of Abraham, and noted also that there was a seventh.

19

Because this seventh rule is the keystone to the Old Testament plan of prosperity, we deferred discussion of it to this present chapter.

What was this Old Testament key to temporal prosperity? The answer is one that all of us should know. It is the law of the tithe, which involves the tenth of our increase. Abraham learned that there was a direct relation between giving the tithe and the enjoyment of temporal prosperity. He recognized and acknowledged that in a peculiar way, one tenth of all he possessed belonged to God, and he was always careful to see that it got into God's hands.

The tithe was instituted for a purpose. Even in that day God had a priesthood to be supported. There was Melchizedek, king of Salem, priest of the most high God. While the kings of the surrounding nations were fighting over possession of the earth, Abraham took time to see that God's ministry was taken care of. Fresh from the battle in which he had defeated Tidal king of nations, Abraham went to the residence of Melchizedek king of Salem, and "gave him tithes of all."

"And Melchizedek king of Salem brought forth bread and wine: and he was the priest of the most high God. And he blessed him, and said, Blessed be Abram of the most high God, possessor of heaven and earth: And blessed be the most high God, which hath delivered thine enemies into thy hand. And he gave him tithes of all" (Gen. 14:18-20).

It was the law of the tithe. Abraham obeyed the law of the tithe and God prospered him. While the kings and princes were seeking wealth by taking it by force, while the inhabitants of Sodom thought they could prosper as they multiplied wickedness, while Lot chose to sit in the gate of Sodom and become a great man in this world, Abraham remembered the law of prosperity and fulfilled his obligation in payment of the tithe. And Abraham prospered and enjoyed riches, temporal and spiritual, for three-quarters of a century after Sodom and Gomorrah had been reduced to ashes!

"And Abram was very rich in cattle, in silver, and in gold" (Gen. 13:2).

"And the Lord hath blessed my master greatly; and he is become great: and he hath given him flocks, and herds and silver, and gold, and menservants, and maidservants, and camels, and asses" (Gen. 24:35).

JACOB AND HIS PROMISE TO GOD (Gen. 28)

We have noted how Jacob had sought the birthright and the blessing, and had taken them by craft and sharp bargaining. But he was to learn that no one steals the blessings of heaven, or at least keeps them, who doesn't play the game according to the rules. All his scheming had gone for naught. He had incurred the hatred of his twin brother, Esau, and was forced to flee for his life. No doubt realizing his folly, and knowing that he would perhaps never see his mother's face again, Jacob did some serious thinking. As night drew on, he stopped at Bethel and laid his head upon a stone that he had set up for a pillow. That night Jacob had his first spiritual experience. During his troubled sleep he had a vision of angels ascending and descending a ladder reaching up to heaven. It was here that he met God for the first time. In the morning he took the stone that he had laid under his head and anointed it. And there he made his covenant with God.

It is at Bethel that we have the first Bible-recorded instance of conversion. It was the conversion of a man who had gotten into trouble. Jacob hardly knew where his next meal was coming from. Would he perish from hunger? Who would clothe him? The precariousness of his situation was very real. But that morning Jacob made a covenant to serve God. Knowing that his grandfather,

Abraham, and no doubt his father, Isaac, had paid tithes, he now made the vow to do likewise. And here was the vow that Jacob made:

"And Jacob vowed a vow, saying, If God will be with me, and will keep me in this way that I go, and will give me bread to eat, and raiment to put on, So that I come again to my father's house in peace; then shall the Lord be my God: And this stone, which I have set for a pillar, shall be God's house: and of all that thou shalt give me I will surely give the tenth unto thee" (Genesis 28:20-22).

Jacob never wanted for bread or for raiment, although he came close to it many times. Actually for his duplicity and trickery he deserved to starve, yet God in His mercy was with him. Though He had to chasten Jacob, and though for many years the man was to reap the results of his misdeeds, God took him through all the way. And the time did come when his trials and tribulations ended. The closing years of his life were blessed indeed. Joseph, his son, brought him down to Egypt to share in his glory and great prosperity.

THE TITHE UNDER THE LAW (Lev. 27:30-31)

The tithe was given under the Law but as we have seen, the tithe did not originate under the Law. It was in existence in the days of Abraham and Jacob and no doubt long before. The tithe was the law of God and therefore with the giving of the Mosaic Law it was only natural that this should be incorporated in it. (Even as for example the law of the sanctity of human life, instituted long before the Law, was included in it Gen. 9:6 and Exod. 20:13.)

And so it was when the Law was given, the commandment concerning the law of the tithe was expressly stated. The tithe or one-tenth was God's to take care of His work.

"And all the tithe of the land, whether of the seed of the land, or of the fruit of the tree, is the Lord's: it is holy unto the Lord. And if a man will at all redeem ought of his tithes, he shall add thereto the fifth part thereof" (Lev. 27:30, 31).

Here is an interesting note: The question is raised as to whether in an emergency one might temporarily borrow part of the tithe. God knew that people, in the midst of financial pressure, would be under temptation to use a part of their tithe, no doubt with good intentions of replacing it later. He knew that in so doing people would find it difficult in many cases to repay what they had borrowed. It was therefore not a good practice. So although God did not forbid borrowing of the tithe, He did set up a safeguard to discourage the practice. If the tithe were borrowed to take care of an emergency, the borrower was not only to repay it, but to add a fifth thereto! That is twenty per cent. Rather high interest! True, but God did not want people appropriating the tithe and then finding themselves under circumstances in which they could not pay it back. He did not want them to bring themselves under the curse which would come if they misappropriated God's money. The fact that God charged interest for the use of the tithe dramatically demonstrates that He considers the tithe as His exclusively.

Why did God regard the tithe as so important? First, the tithe made possible the support of His ministry. And second, the tithe was the key feature in His plan for giving financial security to His people. The tithe could be compared as it were to the premium of an insurance policy. Failure to keep up the premium would cause the policy to lapse. Likewise failure to be scrupulous in the payment of the tithe cancelled God's obligation to provide financial security for the defaultee.

CHAPTER 4

God's Social Security Plan

Today, we are living in an industrialized society. People have come to live in complete dependence on a regular weekly income. If they miss one paycheck they may be in serious financial straits. Because of the nature of our modern economy there has arisen an increasing demand for some kind of social security. Communism has taken advantage of this pressing social problem by making glib promises of a security guaranteed by the state. Communist security, however, has in practice resulted in the loss of all individual liberty, and has been generally recognized as the counterfeit of true security.

In America our government has instituted certain social security laws. In addition we have adopted insurance programs which are playing an ever-increasing role in our economy. Through these means our nation has tried to cushion the shock of financial distresses occasioned as the result of unemployment, sickness, accident, or old age. Notwithstanding these things, fear of the future still plagues millions of people. Runaway inflation, for example, which for years has been a persistent threat, could quickly devalue every insurance policy in America. Our social security reserve is being absorbed by the national deficit and a severe depression could wipe out those assets completely.

THE LAW OF THE CURSE AND THE BLESSING
(Mal. 3)

Long before national social security programs were

ever thought of, God had instituted His own special social security plan. The millions who have adopted this divine plan for their lives have found it has never failed them. Those who rejected or ignored it have been the losers. This plan we refer to is a simple one. It is the law of the tithe as given in Mal. 3:8-10:

"Will a man rob God? Yet ye have robbed me. But ye say, Wherein have we robbed thee? In tithes and offerings. Ye are cursed with a curse: for ye have robbed me, even this whole nation. Bring ye all the tithes into the storehouse, that there may be meat in mine house, and prove me now herewith, saith the Lord of hosts, if I will not open you the windows of heaven, and pour you out a blessing, that there shall not be room enough to receive it."

Notice that these verses are found in the last pages of the Old Testament. The context deals with two main themes. One, the coming of the Lord and events attending the same. And second, it speaks of the purging that God's people must undergo that "they may offer unto the Lord an offering in righteousness (verse 3)." God declares, "I am the Lord I change not" (verse 6). Therefore the divine ordinances are still in force.

And what ordinances are these? Verses 8-10 which follow show that reference is made to none other than the law of the tithe!

Here we are told in definite terms what will happen when that law of the tithe is obeyed, and what happens when it is not.

WILL A MAN ROB GOD?

Many people look upon the tithe as something they give to God. But here we are informed quite differently. The tithe is no more ours than the property that belongs to our neighbor is ours. We hold no right to it, nor are we entitled to any portion of it. We are merely stewards to see that it is brought safely into the house of the Lord.

Moreover, beside the tithe, we are informed that offerings also belong to God. But there is this difference: while the amount of the tithe is fixed, the person himself determines the amount of the offering. He may give little or much as he may decide. Peter, in speaking to Ananias concerning his duplicity in concealing the price obtained from the sale of his property, said, "Whiles it remained, was it not thine own? and after it was sold, was it not in thine own power?" (Acts 5:4). During our lifetime there are certain possessions which we may consider as our own. We may do with them as we choose. We may give generously to God's cause or withhold. In giving offerings, which are above the tithe, we are laying up treasures in heaven. Still, as Peter said, that which is over the tithe is our property, and is in our hands to do with as we see fit.

However, this is not true in the matter of the tithe. The tithe is not ours, even for a moment. It is no more ours than the money handled by the teller at the bank window is his. He is under bond to see that every penny is properly accounted for. No more dare a Christian appropriate the tithe for his own personal use, than may the man take the money he handles at the bank window. If the teller should fail to properly account for funds entrusted to his care, he will, upon the discovery of his peculations, be charged with embezzlement. Upon conviction, he is branded as a criminal, subject to imprisonment.

God says that the person who fails to pay his tithes (and offerings too—although the amount of the offering is left up to the individual) is a robber and worse. If a man robs another man, he commits a crime and the law prescribes severe punishment. But what about the man who robs God? That this is a serious matter is seen from the way the Scripture puts the question. "Will a man rob God?" As if

26

to say, "If a man robs God, how can he hope to escape the judgment of God?" Thieves may sometimes elude punishment. But who can escape from Him whose eye never slumbers or sleeps? We see, therefore, that a man who fails to pay his tithes is, in the sight of God, a thief.

WHAT IS THE PENALTY OF ROBBING GOD?
(Deut. 28)

Why do some dare to rob God? Perhaps the main reason is that God doesn't usually send the punishment immediately.

"Because sentence against an evil work is not executed speedily, therefore the heart of the sons of men is fully set in them to do evil" (Eccles. 8:11).

God is longsuffering. He gets no pleasure from human misery, even when the person suffers as the result of his own misdeeds. And when a man repents and turns from the error of his way, God is quick to forgive and even to blot out the past. So in this case the Lord said of the children of Judah who had withheld the tithe, that if they would turn and do that which was right and honest, "Then shall the offering of Judah and Jerusalem be pleasant unto the Lord, as in the days of old, and as in former years" (Mal. 3:4).

Nevertheless, if they still disobeyed, they would continue to be under the curse. The Scripture speaks plainly, "Ye are cursed with a curse" (Mal. 3:9).

In other words, the hand of God was against these people, whatever they did. In those days the majority of the people lived on the land, and were more or less dependent on what they grew in the field. But the devourer, the worm, had come and destroyed what they planted. The vine cast its fruit before the time.

To understand fully all that the curse involved, we must turn to Deuteronomy 28. Here we find a list of curses, which includes sickness, suffering, famine, defeat in war, and untimely death. Those who violated the law of the Lord, we are told, were cursed in the city and in the field, when they came in and when they came out. Their enemies would come against them and defeat them in battle. They would be taken into captivity and made to serve cruel task masters until they would lament and sigh that life was no longer worth living:

"And thy life shall hang in doubt before thee; and thou shalt fear day and night, and shalt have none assurance of thy life: In the morning thou shalt say, Would God it were even! and at even thou shalt say, Would God it were morning! for the fear of thine heart wherewith thou shalt fear, and for the sight of thine eyes which thou shalt see" (Deut. 28:66, 67).

This, then, was the curse. Robbing God of tithes and offerings invited the curse.

PROVING GOD (Mal. 3)

How can God's people escape the curse and come under blessing? The answer is simple. "Bring ye all the tithes into the storehouse, that there may be meat in mine house" (Mal. 3:10).

And then God adds a very remarkable thing. He invites the people to prove Him. "Prove me now herewith, saith the Lord of hosts." Not often are we told to prove God. But in this case we are invited to actually put the matter to a test and see if obedience to the law of the tithe doesn't pay off. We are to count up those back tithes and bring them into the storehouse and see what happens! See if the curse doesn't go and in its place a blessing come instead— blessings of such abundant measure that there will not be room enough to receive them! See if the windows of heaven will not open, and spiritual, financial, temporal, and physical blessings flow abundantly. "Prove me now herewith, saith the Lord of hosts, if I will not pour you out a blessing, that there shall not be room enough to receive it" (Mal. 3:10).

GIVING TO GOD

How much are we to bring into the storehouse? The tithe comes first—that is the tenth (Gen. 28:22). God stipulates how much our tithe must be. There is no room here for mistake. One tenth of our increase or income is our tithe. But God leaves it up to us as to the size of our offering. How much our offering will be depends on how much faith we have. The widow had faith to give all—and Christ gave her His highest commendation. "Give, and it shall be given unto you" (Luke 6:38). The law of giving is that "He which soweth sparingly shall reap also sparingly; and he which soweth bountifully shall reap also bountifully" (II Cor. 9:6). God gives us an opportunity to act our faith. When we give largely as an act of our faith in God's promise, we show our confidence that God will not fail us. God says to prove Him—prove whether He is God or not. He who proves God will find that the very windows of heaven will open and a blessing will come down greater than he is able to receive.

God has promised to rebuke the devourer. The fruits of the field will no longer be destroyed. The vine will not cast its fruit before the time. And the curse will go. Obedience to the law of the tithe is the royal road that leads to temporal blessings.

EXPERIENCE OF MY PARENTS

My father and mother were people of faith. Father never had a large income, but when he brought his paycheck home, mother would carefully take out the tithe and see that it went into the Lord's work. Having a fairly large family, father's modest income did not provide us with much luxury. Still, none of us suffered. We had plenty to eat and each of us was able to receive a fair education.

Then came the days of the great depression that affected America as no other depression ever had. The stock market plummeted downward and millionaires became paupers overnight. Thousands committed suicide. Soup kitchens were established in the large cities and bread lines appeared. Millions of people, including those who had held prominent places in their communities, were forced to go on relief.

In those days when a man lost his job it was extremely difficult to find another. Many of our neighbors and friends suffered severely during those years of unemployment and hard times. But during that time God's blessing rested upon my parents. Father never lost a day at his job. He was able to pay off the mortgage on his home.

The family benefited in other ways. There were scarcely ever any doctor bills to pay. Once, however, mother became very sick. An examination showed that she had cancer of the stomach. But mother was a woman of great faith. She refused the recommended operation. The miracle took place and she was completely healed! Even while they were praying for her healing, the deliverance came and she vomited up the cancer! Mother lived another twenty years, finally going to be with the Lord on a New Year's day at the age of eighty. And thus did we children have the opportunity in our younger years to learn firsthand the benefits of consistent tithing.

THE AMAZING STORY OF AN EXPERIMENT

One of my friends by correspondence was the late Perry Hayden, who performed an experiment that was publicized over all America. He wanted to prove to people that the law of the tithe was the divine law of prosperity. He decided to plant a cubic inch of wheat and each year tithe the increase. He planted the first crop in the year 1940, and then planted the increase, minus the tithe, the following year. Henry Ford soon became interested in the experiment and furnished the land and equipment for harvesting the crop. But I shall let Mr. Hayden tell the story for it shows the remarkable results possible in a wheat yield when the blessing of God is upon it:

"On Sunday morning, September 22, 1940, I heard a message preached on John 12:24. "Verily, verily, I say unto you, Except a corn of wheat fall into the ground and die, it abideth alone: but IF IT DIE, IT BRINGETH FORTH MUCH FRUIT." Being a miller, and being interested in actually proving God in a rather unique way, I was led to do something the following Thursday that has since been heard of all the way around the world. I planted 360 kernels of wheat (one cubic inch). It takes 2,150 cubic inches to make a bushel, so you can see what a small beginning this project had.

"When we planted the wheat, September 26, 1940, on a plot 4 by 8 feet, I told those present that in 1941 we were going to 'tithe' the crop, and replant it. I was taking Malachi 3:10 seriously and I recommend right now that my reader study this verse as well as the eleventh verse. In Leviticus 25:3 and 4 we find to 'sow the field' for six years and let it rest the seventh; that is what we set out to do.

"In 1941 we cut the 'world's smallest wheatfield.' Immediately, we turned over a tenth of the yield to the local Quaker Church, and replanted the remaining 45 cubic inches in September, 1941.

"In the summer of 1942, we cut the second crop with old-fashioned cradles, and found the yield was 55 fold, or 70 pounds. Again we 'tithed' the wheat and replanted the remaining 63 pounds on land that, for the third year in succession, had been furnished by Henry Ford, who owned a large farm near Tecumseh. In 1943, this acre of land yielded 16 bushels from the one bushel of seed. Henry Ford himself came out to see the wheat cut, and furnished a reaper to cut it and an old-fashioned thresher from his famous Edison Institute Museum at Greenfield Village, to thresh it. Not only that, but Henry again furnished land for the fourth crop. In 1944, this crop on 14 acres yielded 380 bushels. Again, the tenth of the crop was 'tithed' and the remaining cleaned and replanted. Henry Ford furnished the land for the fifth crop. It was 230 acres. In the summer of 1945 a fleet of 40 combines was sent to the field by Ford. The yield from the Dynamic Kernels was 5,555 bushels. The value of this little crop at the market price of $1.55 per bushel, was $8,610.25. The tithe of $861.03 went to the Friends Church who, in turn, gave it to the Tecumseh Hospital.

"And now comes the interesting outcome after Henry Ford had turned over the fifth crop to me. The 5,000 bushels of wheat were sold to approximately 250 farmers in Michigan and nearby states. They had to agree to plant the wheat, and in 1946, to pay a tithe of their crop to their own church. In the summer of 1946 we expected to harvest $100,000 worth of wheat—all from 360 kernels planted six years before, which for five years had been faithfully 'tithed.'

"Mr. Henry Ford's assistance in furnishing land, machines and labor for the first five years was deeply appreciated. And it was all voluntary on his part. How thrilled I was on different occasions when he might visit the wheat field at Tecumseh, or when I might visit him at Dearborn, to hear him say, 'You had faith, didn't you!' or 'You are being led, aren't you?' The very last words Mr. Ford said to me one day after we had visited for possibly an hour, were 'God is within you!' "

CHAPTER 5

Is Tithing for the
New Testament Age?

There yet remains an important question to answer. Is tithing for the New Testament age? This question failed to have significance in the Early Church for one very good reason. The people sold all they had and brought the money and laid it at the apostles' feet! They gave all. During those days they lived in communal style and had all things common. Ordinarily, during the church age, this method has not been found practical. People live better in families than in communals, a system that Communism makes work at the point of a gun. But Christians do not use guns in spreading the Gospel. Communals are not a sound plan for ordinary living. They are for emergencies. People may live together satisfactorily in large numbers during a flood, a disaster, or during a war that sweeps through their land. But after the emergency is over they desire to return to their homes.

In the Early Church there was an emergency. The new Christians were in danger of their lives. A relentless persecution by the Jewish hierarchy kept the infant church in a constant state of jeopardy. The people were glad to live together and enjoy the mutual security that was thus provided. They sold all they had and laid it at the feet of the apostles. However, the time came when circumstances changed and the communal system was abandoned.

For the above reason, tithing was not practiced during

the first few years of the Early Church—simply because the people did not have their separate homes, and they gave all that they had to the church. However, the Scriptures, recognizing that this change would come, and that the communal system was not permanent, plainly taught that tithing was also God's plan during the New Testament age. In these events that took place in the days of the Early Church we find that people, in going beyond the law of the tithe, were discovering the New Testament key to absolute security and the best that God has.

JESUS SAID MEN OUGHT TO TITHE

Jesus spoke on the subject of tithing. He indeed showed that it was not enough to tithe and to omit "judgment, mercy and faith." Just the act of tithing cannot atone for other serious omissions. So that He would not be misunderstood, Jesus commended the fact of tithing but told the Pharisees that they ought to do the other also. "Ye pay tithe of mint and anise and cummin, and have omitted the weightier matters of the law, judgment, mercy, and faith: *these ought ye to have done,* and not to leave the other undone" (Matt. 23:23).

The point we are concerned with here is: Jesus taught that men ought to pay tithes. So far as we know the Pharisees, who tithed, enjoyed material prosperity, although they suffered spiritual loss because of their blindness and inability to recognize the "day of their visitation." Note this: The Lord commended tithing, but showed that there was something more. *That there is something more is a hint that beyond the act of tithing God has a master key for Christian prosperity.*

TITHING IN THE NEW TESTAMENT CHURCH

There are some who insist that tithing has no force in the New Testament Church, and that it is only a part of the Mosaic Law. In this, however, they are mistaken.

Tithing was instituted long before the Law. Both Abraham and Jacob paid tithes.

It is true that tithing, as well as other obligations, is considered in the New Testament as a privilege rather than a command. Believers should do things because they love the Lord rather than because they are forced to do them. Nevertheless, the laws governing prosperity are just as cogent in the New Testament as in the Old. And certainly, if we receive more under grace than under the Law, we should feel as responsible to do as much, *if not more,* than those who lived under the Old Testament.

Nevertheless, that there be no mistake, the Scriptures clearly show that tithing was practiced by the New Testament Church. This is plainly spoken of in Heb. 7:8:

"And here men that die receive tithes; but there he receiveth them, of whom it is witnessed that he liveth."

Note the book of Hebrews was written some 35 years after the institution of the church. The inspired writer says, "Here men that die receive tithes; but there he receiveth them, of whom it is witnessed that he liveth." Thirty-five years passed and ministers still received tithes! But who were those ministers? Is the Scripture here referring to the apostate Jewish religionists who had rejected Christ? Is this tithing that of the followers of the Pharisees who put Christ to death and who attempted to stamp out Christianity? Of course not. Christ Himself is spoken of as receiving the tithes. Money given to the Christ-rejecting Jewish hierarchy could not be said to be received by the Lord. Only that which was given to His ministers could be accepted by Him.

And here is a striking truth. Those who tithe may seem to be giving to man, but indeed their tithes are actually being received and accepted by Christ! They are received by the One "who dieth no more," but lives for evermore!

Thirty-five years after Christ ascended to heaven, acting in His high priesthood after the order of Melchizedek, He received tithes from men. And He still does! How important it is then that as stewards we see that which belongs to Christ is given unto Him. We do not in truth give them to men. Actually the minister is only another steward to whom we give our tithes. They are received by Christ to whom they belong!

GIVING TO CHRIST FOR MISSIONS

There is the story of a missionary who had returned to his home city, where he announced a collection for foreign missions. A good friend said to him: "Very well, Andrew, seeing it's for you, I'll give 100 marks."

"No," said the missionary, "I cannot take the money since you give it seeing me." The man saw the point and said: "You are right, Andrew. Here are 200 marks, seeing it's for the Lord Jesus."

The missionary was right. If the man was to get a blessing out of his giving, he must see Christ as he gave. And how differently we give when we realize that we are indeed giving to Christ!

CHAPTER 6

Riches Under Curse and
Riches Under Blessing

Now that we have seen something of the plan God has given His people by which they may enjoy temporal as well as spiritual prosperity, the question arises: how far a Christian should go in seeking to increase his material possessions? There is a teaching going around in some circles that the size of one's pocketbook is an index to his spiritual status. Surely it would be hard to find a more dangerous teaching than this, nor one that is more clearly repudiated by the Scriptures. The apostle Paul rebukes this gross doctrine of materialism which had apparently gained some followers in his day: "Perverse disputings of men of corrupt minds, and destitute of the truth, supposing that gain is godliness: from such withdraw thyself" (I Tim. 6:5). The fact is that the world has been filled with shipwrecked lives who have lost their experience with God, in a blind race for material gain.

GEHAZI (II Kings 5:20-27)

Gehazi, the servant of Elisha, was one of these. This man had become exceedingly displeased with Elisha's impractical attitude toward money. He had seen how he had refused the gift that Naaman had offered after he had been healed of leprosy. Here had been a great opportunity to replenish the funds of the party, but Elisha had let the opportunity slip by. To Gehazi the chance was too good to be lost. Secretly he follows after Naaman and with a little story which he draws from his imagination he makes a request of Naaman "for a talent of silver and two changes of raiment." Was Gehazi's conscience troubled by this deception? Men have a way of rationalizing their wrongdoings. Gehazi reasoned that he had ministered to Elisha for a long time, and had gotten little enough out of it. Was it not time to take things into his own hands? Elisha need never know how he got the money. Naaman would certainly be pleased with the chance to make the gift. But on his return, Elisha met him with the words:

"Is it a time to receive money, and to receive garments, and oliveyards, and vineyards, and sheep, and oxen, and menservants, and maidservants? The leprosy therefore of Naaman shall cleave unto thee, and unto thy seed forever" (II Kgs. 5:26-27).

Surely the story of Gehazi is a warning against covetousness.

It must be admitted that not a few Christians have a desire to be wealthy. Though they know that the possession of riches is fraught with danger, nevertheless in most cases they are quite willing to assume the risks that might be involved, should a fortune unexpectedly come their way.

It is perhaps true that in the desire for wealth, the motives of people of the world and those of Christians are different. The worlding thinks of the luxury, comfort, and power that money can bring him. The Christian, on the other hand, usually reasons that he could do a great amount of good if only he had unlimited funds at his disposal.

Few, however, consider the warnings that the Bible gives concerning the dangers that confront those who have large possessions. Jesus in His sermon on the Mount gives a stern warning to the rich: "But woe unto you that are rich! for ye have received your consolation" (Luke 6:24). In His parable of the sower, and the seed that fell

38

among the thorns, He showed that those with riches usually brought no fruit to perfection. The "thorns" were "the cares of life and the deceitfulness of riches." The possession of riches is a glittering attraction to people and it seems to promise opportunity to do great good. But in actual practice the person's time and energy is diverted from spiritual things and in the end he usually fails to accomplish anything worthwhile for the kingdom of God. *Only when a man has found the master key to prosperity is he on safe ground in the matter of handling riches.*

A TEMPTATION AND A SNARE

The great apostle Paul gives practically the same warning to those who would be rich:

"But they that will be rich fall into temptation and a snare, and into many foolish and hurtful lusts, which drown men in destruction and perdition. For the love of money is the root of all evil: which while some coveted after, they have erred from the faith, and pierced themselves through with many sorrows. But thou, O man of God, flee these things; and follow after righteousness, godliness, faith, love, patience, meekness" (I Tim. 6:9-11).

These words carry an ominous portent. Riches are not only a snare but they cause people to "err from the faith" and "to fall into harmful lusts." The statement that riches "drown men in destruction and perdition" carries a significance that cannot be ignored. For those who are rich the apostle gives the following solemn admonition:

"Charge them that are rich in this world, that they be not highminded, nor trust in uncertain riches, but in the living God, who giveth us richly all things to enjoy; That they do good, that they be rich in good works, ready to distribute, willing to communicate" (I Tim. 6:17, 18).

The real test of whether a Christian who has wealth is on safe grounds is whether he is "ready to distribute, willing to communicate." This is Bible language for generous giving. If wealthy men have so complicated their affairs that they are not ready nor able to give when the need arises, they are already in the toils of mammon. The fact is that it is not the rich but usually the poor and those in moderate circumstances who pay the cost of spreading the Gospel.

To the rich, James gives a warning that has special reference to these last days:

"Go to now, ye rich men, weep and howl for your miseries that shall come upon you. Your riches are corrupted, and your garments are motheaten. Your gold and silver is cankered; and the rust of them shall be a witness against you, and shall eat your flesh as it were fire. Ye have heaped treasure together for the last days" (James 5:1-3).

THE PARADOX OF RICHES

From the Scriptures that have been quoted it might appear that it is dangerous for any Christian to be rich. *Contradictory as it may seem, we must declare that such a conclusion is quite wrong! The Bible shows that under certain circumstances a Christian may be a man of wealth!* If this seems to be a paradox, let us observe that none other than Jesus Himself affirms the above statement. But we shall also note that such wealth never comes to the Christian because he has pursued riches. It comes to those who have *found and used the master key to prosperity!*

Before we consider what this master key is, let us turn to the words of Jesus who spoke some astonishing things about rich men under the curse and rich men under the blessing.

Despite the apparent advantages of wealth, Jesus made it clear that He regarded riches in the hands of all, except those who had this master key, a dangerous thing to their eternal welfare. In trusting in wealth, man fails to feel his need to trust in God. His whole perspective becomes distorted by the false security of riches. He fails to realize that there are but a few heartbeats between him and the utter loss of all he has. Christ saw hope for the thief when He said, "Today shalt thou be with me in paradise" (Luke 23:43). He saw hope for the publicans and harlots who knew they were sinners. But of a rich man he says, "It is easier for a camel to go through the eye of a needle, than for a rich man to enter into the kingdom of God" (Matt. 19:24).

Christ's attitude toward those who coveted wealth is illustrated in an incident that occurred in His ministry (Luke 12:13-15). A man came to Him asking for justice. According to his story, he had been wronged. He insinuated that his brother, through foul play of some kind, had taken the whole inheritance, including what rightfully belonged to him. Would the Lord speak to his brother, and show him the error of his ways? If the Lord would do this favor, he was certain his brother would be persuaded to return his part of the estate.

But the Lord would do nothing in the case. He did not come to settle petty points of law or differences between relatives. If his brother has stolen what was not his, he would pay the penalty in the end. The man himself still had his honor and his soul—which was the important thing—providing he did not allow himself to get bitter over the matter. However, the Lord showed that if the man permitted the spirit of covetousness to enter in, it could be tragic for him, too.

THE RICH MAN WHO LEFT GOD OUT
OF HIS RECKONING (Luke 12:16-21)

The Lord would drive the lesson home. He told of a rich man who enjoyed great prosperity. His ground brought forth plentifully. His wealth increased until he had no place to take care of his great possessions. He then made a decision. He would pull down his old buildings and build greater. Everything would be the most modern and up-to-date. With wealth and goods laid up for many years, the rich man proposed to really enjoy life. Such a man today would undoubtedly be regarded as a successful business man, a worthy example to follow. Had he not attained wealth through prudence and sound business methods? Nothing at all is inferred that the rich man got his wealth dishonestly. Nevertheless, his great mistake was that he had left God out of his reckoning and calculations.

Christ pointed out the fallacy of the rich man's philosophy. At the moment he was contemplating with complacency his future plans for enlargement of his operations, the sands of his life were about run out. The final hours in which he could make peace with God were swiftly passing, though alas, such thoughts were far from his mind. That same night the rich man ceased to be numbered among the living. In a brief moment of time he was plummeted into eternity!

"But God said unto him, Thou fool, this night thy soul shall be required of thee: then whose shall those things be, which thou has provided? So is he that layeth up treasure for himself, and is not rich toward God" (Luke 12:20, 21).

What happened to the rich man? We can follow this particular individual no longer for his earthly record is finished. Relatives will now divide, perhaps battle, over his property. But he has forever disappeared from the scene. His epitaph has been written by God: "Thou fool, this night thy soul shall be required of thee." Although we cannot follow the destiny of this particular man any further, Jesus has drawn the curtain aside, showing the events that followed the death of another rich man.

A RICH MAN UNDER BLESSING AND A
RICH MAN UNDER CURSE (Luke 16:19-31)

Dives, for so this man is called in ancient records, was also a successful man of wealth. Nothing is said that would suggest that he gained his riches in other than legal ways. Dives knew how to enjoy the good life. Every day he was clothed in the finest of apparel. He was accustomed to the choicest of delicacies. He and his household, which included five brothers, dined sumptuously every day.

But death came to the rich man as it must come to all, and he was suddenly separated from all his wealth.

Christ gives us a brief view of the state of that man in the other world, in hades, the abode of the dead. We see Dives, the rich man, under curse, among the wicked dead without comfort and without hope. On the other side of an impassable gulf is Abraham, a rich man under blessing, with Lazarus, once a beggar at Dives' gate, but now comforted. Dives' position is as intolerable as it is hopeless. The rich man, under the curse, asks Abraham, the rich man under blessing, a favor that Lazarus might return to warn his five brothers against suffering a similar fate. But this is denied him. Since both men in the drama had been rich men on earth, it was not because of riches that Dives was in hades. It was because he made riches his god.

And so Jesus, warning His audience against coveting the riches of this world, showed the solemn fate of those who serve the god of mammon.

THE RICH YOUNG RULER (Mk. 10:17-31)

The Lord was ever consistent in His warning against those who trusted in the riches of this world. One day a young man of position and wealth, but of serious manner, came to Him and asked the question: "Good master, what shall I do that I may inherit eternal life?" (Mark 10:17). The Lord was especially drawn to him, for the narrative says, "Then Jesus beholding him loved´ him." Nevertheless, Christ did not temporize. He replied:

"One thing thou lackest: go thy way, sell whatsoever thou hast, and give to the poor, and thou shalt have treasure in heaven: and come, take up the cross, and follow me" (verse 21).

This was too much for the young man. He went away sad and grieved. As much as he wanted eternal life, he could not find it in his heart to relinquish his great possessions. The Lord looked sadly after him as he went away. Then He spoke to His disciples saying, "Children, how hard it is for them that trust in riches to enter into the kingdom of God!" And then He added, "It is easier for a camel to go through the eye of a needle, than for a rich man to enter into the kingdom of God" (verses 24, 25). This statement so amazed the disciples that they began to say among themselves: "Who then can be saved?" It was then that the Lord made a statement that to the apostles was almost unbelievable. His words must have astonished the disciples even more than anything they had already heard.

For what He said unto them is the master key to both temporal prosperity in this world, and in the world to come. This is the matter discussed in the next chapter.

CHAPTER 7

Christ's Master Key To Prosperity

Christ warned against trusting in riches—and these warnings are among the most solemn in the entire Scriptures. The Lord in fact declared that the pursuit of riches is an almost certain road to soul disaster. He said those who put their trust in mammon have reduced their chances of inheriting the Kingdom of God to the point of their being almost negligible. The warning was so urgent that the disciples, in alarm, had said, "Who then can be saved?" (Matt. 19:25).

What did Jesus mean? Was He putting a premium on poverty? Did He mean that Christians should avoid owning property? Should they spurn all temporal possessions? Must Christians in order to inherit the Kingdom of God give away their property and live as mendicants of a poverty order?

Peter rather sadly remarked to the Lord, "Lo, we have left all, and have followed thee" (Mark 10:28). As if to say, "Lord, if the way of salvation is only through poverty, what about us? We have left all!"

Now comes the Lord's astonishing reply that must have startled the disciples more than anything He had previously said. *Instead of the disciples always being poor, He promised that if they were faithful to their consecration that they would in due season receive an hundredfold of material possessions right here in this life!*

"And Jesus answered and said, Verily I say unto

45

you, There is no man that hath left house, or brethren, or sisters, or father, or mother, or wife, or children, or lands, for my sake, and the gospel's, But *he shall receive an hundredfold now in this time, houses,* and brethren, and sisters, and mothers, and children, *and lands,* with persecutions; and in the world to come eternal. But many that are first shall be last; and the last first" (Mark 10:29-31).

This statement in the light of what the Lord had just taught about riches is so amazing that it demands explanation. Therefore let us note exactly what Jesus has said:

PROMISE OF TEMPORAL WEALTH

"But he shall receive an hundredfold now in this time, houses, and brethren. . . and lands. . ."

There can be no mistake, the promise includes temporal wealth, "houses and lands. . . in this time." How much? An hundredfold! In other words he who gives up thousands in following Christ is eligible to receive hundreds of thousands! Not in the age to come, but this age. *Here then is the master key to prosperity!*

PROMISE FOR ALL BELIEVERS

Moreover, it is to be observed that this remarkable promise of Christ is not reserved for a favored few. "No man that hath left house. . . or lands for my sake and the gospel's, but he shall receive an hundredfold now in this time." God is no respecter of persons. All who fulfill the conditions are eligible for the promise! It is apparent from this that as far as God is concerned, the church could have millionaires among its numbers, enjoying the blessing of God upon their lives. They could receive these temporal blessings in this world, and life eternal in the one to come. Certainly this is a different picture than is usually understood among Christians. Yet from the above statement of the Lord, this conclusion is inescapable.

THE CONDITIONS

Surely these words of Jesus are staggering in their import, and indeed at first appear to be contradictory. For, previously, the Lord had given warnings of the most startling nature against trusting in riches, and the pursuit of the same—warnings that so disturbed the apostles that they wondered if it were possible for anyone to be saved. Then having given them He implies that His disciples can be stewards of the equivalent of hundreds of thousands of dollars of property, or even of millions! What is the explanation of this seeming paradox?

The answer is not as difficult as it first seems. *There are important conditions attached—conditions which must be complied with to prepare the people for this stewardship.*

We must note that it is apparent that God is not interested in making people poor merely for poverty's sake. But He is vitally interested in divorcing His people from trust in riches. As Paul says in I Cor. 7:30, 31 ". . . and they that buy, as though they possessed not; And they that use this world, as not abusing it. . ." God's people may have possessions, but these possessions are not to possess them.

It is sad but true that there are many Christians who are unable to stand prosperity. Such was the case of King Uzziah of Judah, who "was marvelously helped, till he was strong. But when he was strong, his heart was lifted up to his destruction" (II Chron. 26:15, 16).

The riches that Christ promised are to be "received," not eagerly pursued. For it is that love and worship of money that is the root of all evil. Money is so alluring and seems to be able to do so many things. It gives the world what it considers to be security. Its possession is the badge of social success. A poor man is considered a failure, and who wants to be considered a failure? Human vanity is indulged in with the desire to keep up with the neighbors, and money is the means by which this can be done. For these reasons and more, people develop the love for money. The great promise of the hundredfold blessing that Christ has given is only for those who have overcome the evil of this money-love. The Lord meant just what He said when He declared that the promise was for those who in their heart have "left all," and followed Him.

This then is the secret of this amazing promise of Christ. The promise of the hundredfold blessing of "houses and lands" is for those who in their heart have fully given up all these things for the gospel's sake. It does not necessarily mean (although God may lead some to do it) that a man should go out and auction off his goods and give the proceeds to the poor as he asked the rich young ruler to do. *Nevertheless those who make the full consecration to the will of God, sooner or later, will face the test where they may have to consider everything lost, that they might fulfill the will of God.* In one way or another the Lord is going to require each one to prove what He asked Peter to prove, "Lovest thou me more than these?" (John 21:15). It is just here that ninety-nine people out of a hundred fail to become eligible for this great promise. The risk of such absolute consecration to God's will seems too great.

WHY GOD TESTS HIS PEOPLE (Job 1, 2)

Why does God often permit His people to be tested before (or sometimes after) giving them material prosperity? The answer is shown in the story of Job, a godly man whom the Lord had blessed with great riches. Satan had said to God, "Doth Job serve God for naught?" The Lord determined to show the devil, as well as all other subjects of His universe, that there were men who would serve Him whether He prospered them or not. Therefore Satan was permitted for a season to reduce Job to abject poverty. His flocks, his herds, his wealth were all swept away from him. Job's own body was covered with loathsome boils as he, in the very throes of despair, sat on an ashheap scraping himself with a potsherd.

Nevertheless, despite the advice of an ungodly wife who advised him to "curse God and die," Job held fast to his integrity. He thus shut the mouth of Satan, who thought that everyone was such a one as himself. God was able to prove His point and in the end He blessed Job abundantly, restored his health, and gave him twice as much as he ever had before.

Whomever God would trust with wealth, He would first prove, that the man has made his choice to serve God whatever the outcome might be—whether it be in sickness or health, riches or poverty, joy or sorrow.

The supreme test comes as it comes to all who would experience the fulfillment of Christ's promise of the two great blessings—one hundred fold in this life, and in the world to come, life everlasting. As the rich young ruler failed, so many today do likewise. Some gain the material blessings, but lose "life everlasting." Others receive "life everlasting," but their devotion to the utter will of God is not sufficient to make them eligible for great material blessings.

The rich usually fail in fulfilling the conditions that will allow them to do something for the Kingdom of God. Instead of giving in proportion to their real ability when God asks them to give, they tie up their money in speculative investments in hope that they may be able, later, to do something in a grand style. God is displeased by this conduct and does not permit them to succeed because they want to do it their way instead of God's way. Too late they find that they have missed the opportunity that could have been theirs.

Thank God, this is not true of all those who have

means. Some have seen the vision, and have given and continue to give liberally to God's program of winning souls. And God continues to increase their ability to give by pouring more blessings upon them.

USING WEALTH FOR GOD

Those who have pressed through and obtained the promise know that their temporal blessings are not to be used for personal gratification or spent on luxurious living. They realize that in this life they are only stewards— that they are to use what God has given them for the advancement of His Kingdom. And though they realize that they must properly provide for their own, they are not to lay up excessive wealth for their children to later misuse or squander for purposes that may be to their own ruination.

God needs men of means today; men who can give largely to the cause of God. But these must be dedicated men. They must be unawed by their own wealth, humble and consecrated to the entire will of God—men who regard themselves not the owners but the stewards of the temporal blessings God has entrusted to them.

HOW GOD REWARDED US UNEXPECTEDLY

Mrs. Lindsay tells this experience that we had a few years ago:

"It has always been my desire to work hand in hand with my husband, and to be a 'helpmeet' to him—to share with him the burdens of his ministry, to make whatever personal and family adjustments are needed to further the effort of winning lost souls; for the greatest bond that we have had in our marriage is a love for the work of the Lord. Not always has it been easy, nor have I always, immediately, seen eye-to-eye with his vision. In such cases, I have followed along, trusting his better judgment, and believing the Lord would overrule what was not in His perfect will.

"One day I received the surprise of my life when Brother Lindsay came to me, saying he wanted to start a printing plant. 'Start a printing plant? With what?' Such a venture would cost many thousands of dollars, and I knew he had little toward this enterprise.

" 'We could sell our home and use the equity,' was his suggestion.

"Our home! With its one hundred shade trees, where we could come and rest after a busy day at the office. Where our three children had ample space to play; the only thing we could call our own, after years of being on the evangelistic field. 'Sell our home and move where?' 'In the basement apartment of the office,' he replied.

"I also knew that my husband had practically no knowledge of the printing business. What if the venture failed? Would we ever have another home? Would he actually be able to print the millions of faith books and magazines and spread them around the world, as he felt he should?

"For the first few days, I was afraid to pray about the matter. Oh yes, I prayed all around the world. Then one day, the Lord began to speak to my heart. Quickly I drew up an ad for the local paper, and the house was sold the first time the ad appeared!

"Concrete and lumber had to be purchased for the first wing of the printing plant. Soon the building was completed. Equipment had to be purchased. From our equity, we made a down payment on a used press, and also paid for the first carload of paper which cost us $5,700. By now, all our money was gone and we were contentedly living in the basement apartment, for we knew we were in the will of God. Problems arose, having the children so close to the office, with not much space to play, but the Lord helped us.

"After living in these quarters for nearly a year, on a

Saturday morning there came a knock at the door. It was a Christian lady who attended the same church of which the children and I were members. Both she and her husband are contractors. She said, 'My husband was awakened during the night, and said he felt he wanted to build you a house. He wants to donate his service, and will ask his men to do what they can.'

"Build us a house! Who? This man with whom we actually were not acquainted. This man, who made no profession of Christianity, was almost never seen without a large cigar in his mouth, never attended church except once or twice a year—Easter and Christmas—awakened in the middle of the night, to build a house for some preachers! God must be in it!

"To make a long story short, he kept his word. Going to each of his subcontractors, he would say, 'I'm not making a dime on this house, and you aren't either.'

"Soon moving day came! A lovely large brick home, with ample room to entertain the many ministers and missionaries who are associated with the 'winning of the nations.' After the final load of furniture was delivered, I stole away to my bedroom, as the tears of gratitude began to fall, saying, 'Lord, I expected to live in a place like this when I got to heaven, but you gave it to me on earth!' "

"Now unto him that is able to do exceeding abundantly above all that we ask or think, according to the power that worketh in us" (Eph. 3:20).

And today our presses are turning out millions of magazines and faith-building books, for which we praise God!

THE STORY OF C. T. STUDD

When I read of the story of the rich young ruler and its sad ending, I like to think of C. T. Studd, whose niece, Mrs. Walter Michal, a consecrated young Christian lady, was once a member of my congregation. This man's life stands out as a supreme example of proof that it is worthwhile to lose all that the world can offer and to stake everything on the world to come. Born into a rich family, he became converted as the result of the ministry of D. L. Moody. After a period of earnestly seeking God's will, he made his decision to forsake all and follow Christ.

The young convert by nature went all out for everything he loved. In college he played cricket. His brilliant style and resolute nerve made him one of the greatest cricketers of all time. He and his two brothers made a record at Cambridge that has never been equalled. He himself was recognized as the greatest cricketer in England at that time.

One day C. T. Studd read the story of the rich young ruler and was greatly impressed with the words that Jesus spoke to him: "One thing thou lackest; go thy way, sell whatsoever thou hast, and give to the poor, and thou shalt have treasure in heaven: and come, take up the cross, and follow me" (Mark 10:21). After carefully pondering the matter he made an irrevocable decision. He would give away his fortune and become a missionary to China!

The Studd family was very wealthy. When his father died, Charley's share alone was reckoned at about $150,-000. All this he planned to give away when he reached the age of twenty-five. Christ had promised him an hundred fold, and that meant 10,000 per cent—a good investment, he thought. As coolly and deliberately as a business man invests in "gilt-edged" securities, Charley Studd invested in the bank of heaven. He sent $25,000 to Mr. Moody; $25,000 to George Muller for his orphanage; $25,000 went to help the poor in London; $20,000 was given to missionary work. He kept about $16,000 in his own possession and gave it to his bride. But she said, "Charley, didn't the Lord tell you to give all?" So that went to

General Booth and certain others who he was assured were doing a worthy work on the field.

Did God keep His promise? It is too long a story to tell here. But the facts are that in twenty years God sent him nearly three-quarters of a million dollars for missionary work! The crusade he began grew until it was able to support hundreds of missionaries. God performed wonders for C. T. Studd. His wife, who was on an invalid's couch, got up healed by a mighty miracle. Studd was honored by kings. On one occasion he was made "Chevalier of the Royal Order of the Lion" by the king of Belgium for his services in the Congo. But best of all he saw his vision catch fire among the people with whom he worked. Before he died he had the joy of witnessing revival fires spreading into many lands. The life of C. T. Studd, son of one of the richest men of England, once reckoned as the greatest cricketer of all time who gave up all that he might win for Christ, is proof that the words of Jesus and His master key to prosperity in this world and the one to come, really work.

DAILY DEPENDENCE

There is one thing we must always remember. No matter how much God may bless His people with material blessing, He wants them always to remain in daily dependence upon Him. Though hundreds of thousands of dollars may pass through the hands of some of His stewards, He usually never gives a large surplus so that His people can be at ease in Zion. He gave oil in the pot to Elisha as long as it was being poured out. When there were no more vessels to receive the oil, it stayed (II Kings 4:6). God would have His people to be as the Israelites of old, who though they were given angel's food, were not permitted to hoard it. They had to gather it afresh each day. God would have our prayer always be the one Jesus taught us, "Give us this day our daily bread" (Matt. 6:11).

CHAPTER 8

The Problem of Poverty

In considering the subject of temporal blessings and their relation to the Christians, we dare not ignore the obvious fact that some of God's people are poor, and that many of these are devoted followers of the Lord. How can we reconcile this fact with God's law of prosperity?

Now whatever is said on this subject, one thing should be made clear. God has a tender regard for the poor and will not overlook any ill treatment of them. He who would look upon the poor with contempt or disdain must incur the displeasure of God:

"He that oppresseth the poor reproacheth his Maker: but he that honoureth him hath mercy on the poor" (Proverbs 14:31).

James observed that the people in the Hebrew Church were beginning to show special favors to the rich (James 2:6). The wealthy were being given undue prominence, while the poor were being made to feel that they were not welcome (James 2:2, 3). The apostle considered this a great evil. And then he showed that the poor, although lacking in material things and perhaps the ability to accumulate them, were nevertheless rich in faith:

"Hearken, my beloved brethren, Hath not God chosen the poor of this world rich in faith, and heirs of the kingdom which he hath promised to them that love him?" (James 2:5).

For this reason the Scriptures abound in admonitions concerning our obligations to the poor and that we must never take advantage of them or oppress them.

Nevertheless we must consider this question. In view of

God's promises of prosperity to His people, why does it happen that many devout Christians still have had to wrestle with poverty? How can we reconcile the fact of poverty in many cases with the great Bible promises of prosperity?

Now the truth of the matter is that there is more than one reason why some of God's people are poor. A knowledge of these reasons is important if we are to keep the right spirit in our judgment of the poor and the causes of their poverty.

1. SOME CHOOSE POVERTY THAT THEY MIGHT BE OF GREATER SERVICE TO GOD

When Christ was born into this world He came not to a palace, but instead shared a stable with the animals. He deliberately refused the pomp and affluence of wealth, and in His great condescension became poor that others might become rich!

"For ye know the grace of our Lord Jesus Christ, that, though he was rich, yet for your sakes he became poor, that ye through his poverty might be rich" (II Cor. 8:9).

The Apostle Paul, in initiating a missionary ministry to the gentiles, found that he could reach them in the most effective way if he became as they were—if he would share their burdens, their sorrows, their distresses and their poverty. While Paul, because of his great education and brilliant intellect, could have gone to the top of almost any profession he might have chosen, he rather determined to count all things loss that he might win Christ. And so Paul knew poverty. Yet at times Paul was liberally provided for. He knew "both how to be abased, and. . . how to abound" (Phil. 4:12). On occasions he was steward of large sums of money which he used to help the poor and extend the gospel. Paul sums up his experience in II Cor. 6:10:

"As sorrowful, yet always rejoicing; as poor, yet making many rich; as having nothing, and yet possessing all things."

THE POOR MAN OF ASSISI

Saint Francis, the poor man of Assisi, stands out as a shining light in a dark age when the clergy had become corrupt and dissolute. He lived in a day when temporal things engaged the full attention of men, to the tragic loss of spiritual values. But Francis had heard from heaven, and his deep desire to help the people caused him to make an unusual vow before God to live in such a way as to show the world that there was something more valuable than gold. In this vow, he renounced all worldly possessions. He and his followers went out two by two and preached the Gospel of the Kingdom in the same simple way that the apostles had done in the days of Jesus. And the fact is that no man of his time made such an impact upon the world. God did not demand that St. Francis live a life of poverty. He followed such a life because of his love for God and his generation. It was the sincere devotion and utter consecration to the Lord of this humble servant of God that moved kings and popes. After he died the friars that carried on the order still had their poverty, but it was only a form. They accomplished little because they lacked the burning love for the souls of men that their leader had.

2. SOME CHRISTIANS GO THROUGH A SPECIAL TIME OF TESTING

Those who would have the hundred-fold blessings that Jesus promised His disciples need not expect that they will overnight become possessors of wealth. There comes first the forsaking of all. Abraham left all before he received all. Many of God's saints who are in prosperous circumstances today can well recall the period of their testing. There are ministers who can probably remember the time when they had to get along on pennies. Perhaps at the time they felt a little envious, when some of their friends took prosperous pastorates at liberal salaries, while they, trying to obey God's will, labored in new fields where the material rewards were small. Today, they still remember those trials and sacrifices, but with pleasure rather than regret. For while in those circumstances they learned to lean heavily on God. Having resigned themselves to modest living, or even poverty, it came perhaps as a surprise when God turned their "captivity" and began to pour His temporal blessings upon them. Remember the story of Job!

3. MATERIAL BLESSINGS ARE ONLY TEMPORAL

We must not forget that material blessings are only temporal and subject to the decay of this age. Our true possessions are in "that city whose builder and maker is God." Today we are living at the eve of great dispensational changes. Nations and kingdoms are falling. With the coming of atomic power there is the threat that the very foundations of society will be laid bare. Here in America we yet enjoy liberty and religious freedom. Nevertheless, in some countries believers serve God at the risk of their lives. The evil threat of communism has cast its shadow over the entire world. Can we honestly promise the Christians who live behind the Iron Curtain material prosperity and an abundance of the good things of life? Indeed under the anti-god dictatorship that they live with, they are grateful to survive from one day to another.

We repeat, we are at the eve of great world changes. Developments are moving fast in the communist countries, making way for the reign of the very Antichrist. God's judgments may soon come upon America as well as all other countries. What then shall we say concerning those who look covetously at the riches of this world? God's word of advice to Baruch in a similar time of judgment is timely advice for us today. Baruch had been Jeremiah's servant. He had risked his life in being faithful to God's cause. Now he was asking himself what he was going to get out of it. But the Lord sent a message to Baruch. He told him that this was not the hour to seek great things for himself. For the time had come when the nations, including Israel, were to be plucked up and thrown down. Nevertheless because he had been faithful, the Lord would remember him. While the masses perished or went into captivity, God's hand of protection would be upon him wherever he went.

"Thus shalt thou say unto him, The Lord saith thus; Behold, that which I have built will I break down, and that which I have planted I will pluck up, even this whole land. And seekest thou great things for thyself? seek them not; for, behold, I will bring evil upon all flesh saith the Lord: but thy life will I give unto thee for a prey in all places whither thou goest" (Jer. 45:4, 5).

It is interesting to note that those who remained to inherit the land of Israel following the judgment that fell on the nation were the "poor of the land."

Nevertheless, we must admit that there are those who are in poverty because they have neglected God's law, and we shall briefly take note of these cases.

4. POVERTY CAUSED BY DISREGARD OF THE LAW OF THE TITHE.

As several chapters have been given to discussion of the law of the tithe and its relation to the believer's prosperity, we need only mention the law of the tithe here. Suffice it to repeat that many Christians who are in dire circumstances are in that condition because they have robbed God and have taken the tithe which belongs to Him. No Christian can appropriate what belongs to God and expect to prosper. He is cursed with a curse and he can expect poverty as well as other misfortunes.

5. POVERTY CAUSED BY SHIFTLESSNESS

What we say here is a common observation and needs to be mentioned briefly. Careless Christians, like the prodigal son, can waste their substance and come to poverty. This is far different from giving to the cause of Christ as did C. T. Studd. Moreover, some people are afflicted with laziness and to them the slightest effort is an inconvenience. As regards those given to indolence, Paul said, "If any would not work, neither should he eat" (II Thes. 3:10). The writer of the Proverbs also had this to say:

"Yet a little sleep, a little slumber, a little folding of the hands to sleep: So shall thy poverty come as one that travelleth, and thy want as an armed man" (Proverbs 6:10, 11).

Few will disagree here. Those who disobey God's command to work, and who spend their time in idleness can expect poverty. God's law of prosperity is for the obedient. True believers are those who are "not slothful in business" (Rom. 12:11), but are up and about their Master's business.

6. POVERTY BECAUSE GOD CANNOT TRUST SOME WITH WEALTH

It is sad but true that God cannot trust some of His people with too much prosperity. Agur, son of Jakeh, offered the following prayer asking that God give him neither poverty nor riches:

"Remove far from me vanity and lies: give me neither poverty nor riches; feed me with food convenient for me: Lest I be full, and deny thee, and say, Who is the Lord? or lest I be poor, and steal, and take the name of my God in vain" (Proverbs 30:8, 9).

The story of the Bible includes a record of many who could not stay humble when God prospered them. God blessed Lot. But in his desire to increase his wealth he became partner with the wicked of Sodom. Being warned by angels of impending judgment, he fled just in time to escape the doomed city. But the balance of his days were spent in poverty in the mountains.

Israel received the great promises of prosperity, but Moses, looking forward in the spirit of prophecy, foresaw that when prosperity came, they would forsake God.

"But Jeshurun waxed fat, and kicked: thou art waxen fat, thou art grown thick, thou art covered with fatness; then he forsook God which made him, and lightly esteemed the Rock of his salvation" (Deut. 32:15).

Saul was a young man with so many noble and excellent qualities that he was chosen to be the first king of Israel. Yet when God exalted him to this position of honor, he became proud of heart and utterly failed.

David was blessed as no other king in Israel, but when he felt he had reached the pinnacle of success, he·committed his great sin.

Solomon in the early days of his reign was a humble king, who asked God for wisdom rather than riches. When, however, riches and great prosperity came to him, his heart was turned away from the Lord.

Hezekiah was one of Judah's truly great kings. Through his prayers his nation was delivered, and he himself was recovered from an illness that, except for a miracle, would surely have proved fatal. Yet after this great deliverance, Hezekiah's heart became lifted up and he failed to walk with the Lord as he had done before.

"But Hezekiah rendered not again according to the benefit done unto him; for his heart was lifted up:

therefore there was wrath upon him, and upon Judah and Jerusalem" (11 Chron. 32:25).

Many more such incidents could be mentioned. Prosperity seems to have an adverse spiritual effect on all except those who have a sound spiritual foundation. How many, after a little prosperity, have faltered. That God should prevent some from attaining all that they desire in the way of material things is perhaps one of His greatest acts of mercy.

7. POVERTY BECAUSE OF FAILURE TO CLAIM THE PROMISES OF GOD

Wealth is produced through industry. Sick people are unable to work, or at least to work effectively. As a result many, because of illness, are in poverty. But God has promised health for the Christian. Even under the law, the obedient believer was promised deliverance from sickness.

"And ye shall serve the Lord your God, and he shall bless thy bread, and thy water; and I will take sickness away from the midst of thee" (Ex. 23:25).

The Psalmist tells us there was not one feeble one among the tribes:

"He brought them forth also with silver and gold: and there was not one feeble person among their tribes" (Psalm 105:37).

In the New Testament the same standard of health is indicated:

"Beloved, I wish above all things that thou mayest prosper and be in health, even as thy soul prospereth" (III John 2).

Unfortunately, there are thousands of Christians who are in poverty for no other reason than that Satan has taken advantage of them as he did the woman in the synagogue (Luke 13:16) and has bound them with physical afflictions, so they cannot properly carry out the responsibilities of life.

How sad is the story we often hear. People have lost their jobs. Doctor and hospital bills have mounted up. They are like the little woman that came to Christ who had an issue of blood for twelve years and who "had spent all her living upon physicians, neither could be healed of any" (Luke 8:43). Many good people are in poverty for the identical reason this woman was. What is the answer to their problem? They should do the same as she did: press through, until they have touched the hem of the garment of Christ!

OVERCOMING POVERTY

The problem of poverty can be solved. Mrs. Lindsay tells an interesting story of how her sister rose from a battle with poverty to prosperity and blessing:

"We were a large family, and as is often the case, my older sister married young. Her husband had no particular occupation or profession. His jobs would generally last no longer than a few months. Times were hard for a couple so young.

"But the picture has a bright side. My sister was a most devout Christian, a prayer warrior, and *consistent tither*. I actually believe that she'd have lived on bread and water before she'd have taken one cent that belonged to God.

"The depression came! Jobs were even more difficult to find. My sister, always industrious, moved with her husband and daughter into an apartment of a church in the city in which she lived, to become its custodians. She took real pride in keeping the church spotless, while her husband kept up the repairs. At the same time, the young daughter was able to spend hours practicing on the church organ.

"One Christian virtue that has always stood out in my sister's life was her generosity to evangelists, missionaries, pastors and the needy in general. Her apartment was constantly alive with those with whom she shared what she had. How well do I remember the many times we passed through her hometown early in our ministry, when she would have a coat for me, a dress, or some item for the children. I was her sister. But she didn't stop there. How she helped so many with the little she had, I shall never know. It looked many times like the multiplying of the loaves and fishes in the Bible story.

"The years have come and gone. What have they brought? In place of the church apartment, my sister and her husband now own a string of rental houses. My sister and her husband could retire. But no! 'The more God blesses us, the more money we have to put back into the Lord's work,' she says. The daughter? For several years she conducted a radio broadcast for the young people, playing, singing and preaching. Today, she and her husband with their two lovely children are serving as missionaries in French West Africa."

"No good thing will he withhold from them that walk uprightly" (Psalm 84:11).

CHAPTER 9

Should the Poor Be Encouraged to Give?

One of the most important things that Jesus taught about giving concerned the poor. We sometimes suppose that we have done the magnanimous thing when we excuse from giving those who are in poor circumstances. But not Jesus. He took opportunity to show in the most impressive way that God honored and encouraged giving, even by the poorest person. And also that God is not impressed so much by the size of the gift, but rather by the spirit of the giver.

THE WIDOW'S TWO MITES (Luke 20:47; 21:1, 2)

Toward the close of His ministry the Lord one day came into the temple and sat down to observe those who were giving. (And incidentally, Christ always watches our giving, accepting it or rejecting it, in accordance with the spirit and motive in which the gift is given.) He had just severely rebuked the scribes who professed religion as a coverup for their crooked dealing—taking advantage of even the poor widows, foreclosing on their homes and turning them out into the street. He had severely condemned these hypocrites, pointing out that their deeds were the more contemptible since they were done in the name of religion. Here as always, the Lord's solicitude and compassion for the poor was evident.

Now at that very moment the Lord took note of one of those widows who had just dropped her last two mites into the temple treasury (Luke 21:2). While He watched her, He also saw the rich people who were casting substantial gifts into the treasury box. Compared to these gifts, the widow's mites appeared trifling. To some it would have seemed fitting had the Lord deterred the woman and cautioned her that under her present circumstances it was unwise for her to give all the money she had. Should she not keep her little offering to meet her own needs, especially as there were many rich people giving so generously? Even the scribes would concur in such advice. But did the Lord say this? Not at all! Instead, He commended the woman for her gift and had it recorded so that her act would be known to all generations to come! Moreover He declared that her gift of two mites was more in the sight of God than that of all the others who had given! "Of a truth I say unto you, that this poor widow hath cast in more than they all: For all these have of their abundance cast in unto the offerings of God: but she of her penury hath cast in all the living that she had" (Luke 21:3, 4).

But what about this poor widow? How would she live, now that she had nothing left? She herself little realized that the Lord of heaven at that moment had been sitting there watching her act. She had given solely because she wanted at least a tiny part in the work of the Lord. But we ask, had she given to a God who would remember her only in the next world and who had not made provision for her here on earth? The record tells us no more of her story. But we know what must have happened. For the Lord had said, "Give and it shall be given unto you." That is the principle of the Kingdom of God. And the Scriptures cannot be broken. God's blessing would be upon her two mites, and His blessing would be upon her.

THE WIDOW WHO FED ELIJAH (I Kgs. 17:8-16)

This same lesson is taught in the Old Testament in the story of the widow who fed Elijah. She had just meal and oil enough for one last cake for her son and herself. They would eat and die. But Elijah said, "Make me therefore a little cake first, and bring it unto me, and after make for thee and for thy son" (I Kings 17:13). The story is a familiar one. She made a cake for Elijah and then for herself and her son, "and the barrel of meal wasted not, neither did the cruse of oil fail," until the day the Lord sent rain upon the earth (verses 14-16).

From this we see that God encourages all His people to give. Even the poorest cannot afford not to give, for in their giving is the assurance that God will supply their needs. Even the converted heathen of foreign fields needs to be taught this. Perhaps one of the greatest mistakes made in these lands has been the assumption that the people are too poor to give, or to pay their tithes. This is very wrong indeed and it cheats the people out of the blessings God intends for them. Therefore we need not hesitate or flinch from teaching the poor as well as the rich to give to God's work. We are not to hesitate in accepting their offering, even if it appears in the eyes of some that they are giving too much. Surely the poor need the blessing of God as much as do those with large means.

CHAPTER 10

The Hour of Decision

What then must you do to receive the temporal blessings that God intended you to have? Blessings which will enable you to contribute largely to the gospel work? It is hardly necessary to repeat what has already been said. See that your tithe, without fail, goes into the Lord's storehouse. Exercise faith in your giving, as you do when you come to God for other purposes. As you present your tithe or offering, reckon that you are presenting it to Christ who, according to Heb. 7:8, receives it from your hand. When you asked the elders to pray for your healing, you knew that your faith must be in God, that He alone could hear your petition. So when you bring your tithes or offerings, let it be an act of faith, not of giving unto men, but unto God.

CHANGING EARTHLY TREASURES
INTO HEAVENLY TREASURES

"Lay not up for yourselves treasures upon earth, where moth and rust doth corrupt, and where thieves break through and steal: But lay up for yourselves treasures in heaven, where neither moth nor rust doth corrupt, and where thieves do not break through nor steal (Matt. 6:19, 20).

Hence when God gives His people material prosperity it is not that they should accumulate riches so they can speculate on a large scale. . . or greedily seek after still greater wealth. But rather that as God prospers them, they should give generously and consistently to His cause

(I Cor. 16:2). Do not put off your giving to some future time, when you think that you will make a great financial strike. Give now! Money given to God carries a hundred-fold interest. (That is 10,000 per cent!) Is there an investment in which you can do better?

LARGE SUMS ARE NEEDED FOR WORLD EVANGELIZATION NOW

It is sometimes thought that the apostles of the Early Church carried out their task of world evangelization without funds. This is far from the truth. It was true, that for a certain reason, the Lord at the beginning of His ministry told the disciples not to provide gold or silver in their purses. However, at the end of His ministry, Christ changed that command. Although He did prove He could supply their need supernaturally, providing money from even the fishes' mouths, yet He did not intend that His disciples should become sort of mystery men who travelled over the country living without visible means of support. This would only result in people getting unreal and impractical ideas about God's plan for His ministry. It would cause them to fail to do their part in the work of the Lord. So although Christ, at the beginning of His ministry told His disciples not to take a purse or scrip with them, He now commands them to do that very thing.

"And he said unto them, When I sent you without purse, and scrip, and shoes, lacked ye anything? And they said, Nothing. Then said he unto them, But now, he that hath a purse, let him take it, and likewise his scrip: and he that hath no sword, let him sell his garment, and buy one" (Luke 22:35, 36).

The actual fact is that immediately after the birth of the church, large sums of money were placed in the hands of the apostles. People sold all that they had and laid the proceeds at their feet.

"And with great power gave the apostles witness of

the resurrection of the Lord Jesus: and great grace was upon them all. Neither was there any among them that lacked: for as many as were possessors of lands or houses sold them, and brought the prices of the things that were sold, And laid them down at the apostles' feet: and distribution was made unto every man according as he had need" (Acts 4:33-35).

Note that this giving of large gifts in the Early Church was in connection with the message of the apostles' witnessing of the Resurrection, and the fulfillment of the command of Christ to preach the Gospel to every creature:

"But ye shall receive power, after that the Holy Ghost is come upon you: and ye shall be witnesses unto me both in Jerusalem, and in all Judaea, and in Samaria, and unto the uttermost part of the earth" (Acts 1:8).

The funds given at the beginning were not immediately used to evangelize distant areas, for the first task was to evangelize Jerusalem. After that they went to the nearby Judean cities, and then Samaria, and finally to the uttermost parts of the earth.

Likewise today, as with the Early Church, the great responsibility of world evangelization lies before us. But for two reasons, our responsibility is incalculably greater. It is estimated that the population of the world that will live and die during a lifespan in this twentieth century is equivalent to all the generations since the time of Christ! By 1980, the population will be over four billion! Yet as recently as the 14th century, world population was only seventy-five million, a third of which died in the black death. The other reason is that although the Early Church had the whole age before them to evangelize, today it is a race against time. The threat of atomic destruction in another war means that what we do we must do quickly.

As in the Early Church there is a similar need today of heroic giving. We must reach the heathen with the Gospel in large numbers. And afterwards we must take care of the converts by providing buildings and shelters for them, where they can continue to worship God after the large meetings are over. And so the command comes to us today as it came to the disciples of the Lord, and to those of the Early Church:

"So likewise, whosoever he be of you that forsaketh not all that he hath, he cannot be my disciple" (Luke 14:33).

TURNING YOUR TREASURES
INTO HEAVENLY RICHES

How can you get the greatest return for your money? Jesus in the story of the unjust steward gave the answer (Luke 16). Notice that Jesus did not commend this steward for his previous wrongdoing. He called him an unjust steward. However, there is an important lesson to be learned from this parable. The unjust steward saw that he was soon to be put out of his stewardship. As he thought of the future, he realized that he had made little or no preparation for it. Therefore, while he was able, he decided to exercise his office of stewardship in making friends of his Lord's debtors. This he did by reducing the amount they owed, giving them opportunity to clear their indebtedness. Jesus commenting said, "The children of this world are in their generation wiser than the children of light" (Luke 16:8).

From this parable the Lord drew a word of advice:

"And I say unto you, Make to yourselves friends of the mammon of unrighteousness; then, when ye fail, they may receive you into everlasting habitations" (Luke 16:9).

What did the Lord mean by this? Simply that we are to use our means, which is "the mammon of un-

71

righteousness," for the cause of winning souls into the Kingdom of God. One by one these souls will leave this life to be with Christ in "the everlasting habitations." There in glory the redeemed will be made to know who it was who labored, who prayed, who gave of their means for their salvation. There will be welcome parties for the saints as they go marching home! Some perhaps did not have the privilege to go out and preach the Gospel. But they took of their means and made it possible for others to go, and in this way they were able to win a great number of souls. For these people there will be a great welcome! The courts of heaven will ring with shouts of joy as those generous Christian givers are welcomed into the "eternal habitations."

How is your money being used while you are alive? How will it be used after you are gone? Are you leaving some of your possessions for God's work, or shall all you have be left for others to squabble over, even as some did in the days of Jesus (Luke 12:13)? You are the one to make the decision! And *now* is the time to make it. It is the one way you can take it with you!